From B

CATULLUS

A Phoenix Paperback

This abridged edition published in 1996 by Phoenix
a division of Orion Books Ltd
Orion House, 5 Upper St Martin's Lane, London
WC2H 9EA

ISBN 1 85799 5635

Typeset by Deltatype Ltd, Ellesmere Port, Cheshire
Printed in Great Britain by Clays Ltd, St Ives plc

2

Sparrow, my Lesbia's darling pet,
Her playmate whom she loves to let
Perch in her bosom and then tease
With tantalising fingertips,
Provoking angry little nips
(For my bright beauty seems to get
A kind of pleasure from these games,
Even relief, this being her way,
I think, of damping down the flames
Of passion), I wish I could play
Silly games with you, to ease
My worries and my miseries.

O Venus and you Cupids, shed
A tear, and all in man that's moved
By beauty, mourn. Her sparrow's dead,
My darling's darling, whom she loved
More than she loves her own sweet eyes,
Her honey of a bird. It knew
Its mistress as babes recognise
Their mothers, and it never flew
Out of her lap, but all day long,
Hopping and flitting to and fro,
Piped to her private ear its song.
Nevertheless, now it must go
Down the dark road from which they say
No one returns. Curse you, you spiteful
Swooping hawks of death who prey
On all things that make life delightful! –
That was a pretty bird you took.
Bad deed! Poor little bird – by dying
See what you've done! Her sweet eyes look
All puffed and rosy-red with crying.

My Lesbia, let us live and love
And not care tuppence for old men
Who sermonise and disapprove.
Suns when they sink can rise again,
But we, when our brief light has shone,
Must sleep the long night on and on.
Kiss me: a thousand kisses, then
A hundred more, and now a second
Thousand and hundred, and now still
Hundreds and thousands more, until
The thousand thousands can't be reckoned
And we've lost track of the amount
And nobody can work us ill
With the evil eye by keeping count.

She must be ugly, dull and gross
Or else you wouldn't be so close,
Flavius; you'd talk to me – you'd not
Be able not to. But you've got
Some scabrous little slut, and shame
Gags you – you won't tell me her name.
That bed, though dumb, refutes your claim
Of love-starved bachelor nights: the scented
Syrian oil, the wreaths, the dented,
Disordered cushions – they're all speaking
Against you; why, the frame's still creaking
And tottering groggily on its pins.
It's pointless to hush up your sins
When those exhausted, shagged-out flanks
Show you've been up to foolish pranks.
So, good or bad, give me the news.
Catullus and his frivolous Muse
Are longing to apotheosise
You and your 'goddess' to the skies.

How many kisses satisfy,
How many are enough and more,
You ask me, Lesbia. I reply,
As many as the Libyan sands
Sprinkling the Cyrenaic shore
Where silphium grows, between the places
Where old King Battus's tomb stands
And Jupiter Ammon has his shrine
In Siwa's sweltering oasis;
As many as the stars above
That in the dead of midnight shine
Upon men's secrecies of love.
When he has all those kisses, mad-
Hungry Catullus will have had
Enough to slake his appetite –
So many that sharp eyes can't tell
The number, and the tongues of spite
Are too confused to form a spell.

Enough, Catullus, of this silly whining;
What you can see is lost, write off as lost.
Not long ago the sun was always shining,
And, loved as no girl ever will be loved,
She led the way and you went dancing after.
Those were the days of lovers' games and laughter
When anything you wanted she approved;
That was a time when the sun really shone.
But now she's cold, you too must learn to cool;
Weak though you are, stop groping for what's gone,
Stop whimpering, and be stoically resigned.
Goodbye, my girl. Catullus from now on
Is adamant: he has made up his mind:
He won't beg for your favour like a bone.
You'll feel the cold, though, you damned bitch, when men
Leave *you* alone. What life will you have then?
Who'll visit you? Who'll think you beautiful? Who'll
Be loved by you? Parade you as his own?
Whom will you kiss and nibble then?

                                    Oh fool,
Catullus, stop this, stand firm, become stone.

Veranius, my dear friend, the friend worth
More to me than three hundred thousand others,
Is it true that you've come back to home and hearth,
To your old mother and affectionate brothers?
It's true. Wonderful news! In a short while
I'll see you safe and well, hear you describe
In your inimitable traveller's style
The sights of Spain, a landscape or a tribe,
Put my arms round you, draw you close and then
Plant on the mouth and eyes I love a kiss.
Of all the world's supremely happy men
Who is as happy as Catullus is?

I was in the Forum once at a loose end
When I was seized and hauled off by my friend
Varus to meet his girl. 'A prostitute,'
I thought at the first glance, 'but rather cute,
In fact quite pretty.' Soon talk started flowing
On various topics. Then: 'How are things going
In the province of Bithynia these days? Is it
Prospering? Are you richer for your visit?'
I told the simple truth: that no one there
Can line his pocket or perfume his hair –
That goes for natives, governors and staff too,
Especially if you're in the retinue
Of some mean sod who doesn't give a thought
To his employees. 'But at least you brought
The local product back,' they said – 'a litter
With litter-men?' I, trying hard to glitter
In the girl's eyes, said, 'Oh, things weren't so bad,
Despite the rotten province that I had,
That I can't call my own eight sturdy-backed
Good litter-men. (I hadn't one, in fact,
There or in Rome, on whom I could rely
To hoist a broken bed-leg shoulder-high!).
At which the girl, just like a cheeky tart,

Said, 'Dear Catullus, could you bear to part
For an hour with them? I only want a ride
To the temple of Serapis.' 'Steady!' I cried.
'I meant to say . . . well, strictly, I was wrong
To call them *my* slaves. Actually, they belong
To a friend of mine who purchased them – that is,
To Gaius Cinna. Anyway, mine or his,
It's all the same to me; I have the loan;
I use them just as though they were my own.
But you're a tactless nuisance. It's absurd
To take a man up on a casual word.'

Furius and Aurelius, loyal comrades,
Who'd travel with me to remotest India,
Where the beaches pounded by the Eastern Ocean
    Boom to the rollers' thud,

Into Hyrcania, languorous Arabia,
Among the Scythians or the archer Parthians,
Or to the plains which Nile, the seven-tongued river,
    Darkens with churned-up mud,

Who'd march on foot across the Alpine passes
To view the trophy-sites of mighty Caesar,
The Rhine in Gaul, or the outlandish Britons
    Fenced by their sullen strait –

Staunch friends, ready to share all hazards with me,
Anything that the will of heaven proposes,
Please take this message to my girl, a few short
    Words to express my hate:

Good luck to her, let her enjoy her lovers,
The whole three hundred that she hugs together,

Loving none truly, by grim repetition
    Wringing them all sperm-dry.
Let her not look to find my love unaltered;
Through her own fault it lies in ruins, fallen
Like a wildflower at a field's edge that the ploughshare
    Touches and passes by.

Fabullus, if the gods are kind,
In a few days you'll be wined and dined
At my house – if it's understood
You bring the feast with you: good food,
Good wine, a pretty girl, salt wit,
And lots of laughs to garnish it.
Those are the terms of my fine dinner,
Sweet friend, for the old cobweb-spinner
Is busy in my purse. My side
Of the bargain will be to provide
The most delicious of all presents
Imaginable, love's pure essence –
The ointment which was my girl's gift
From Venus and the Loves. Once sniffed,
You'll beg the gods to metamorphose
Fabullus into one huge nose!

Aurelius, I'm entrusting you with all
I love most, with my boy. I ask a small
Favour. If you have ever pledged your soul
To keep some cherished object pure and whole,
Then guard him – I don't mean from any stranger
Walking the streets on business bent: the danger
I fear is you yourself and that great spike
That ruins good and naughty boys alike.
When you're outside the house, wave your erection
At any one you like, in what direction
You please, but (I'm not asking much, I trust)
Make him the one exception. If, though, lust
And sheer perversity unhinge your reason
And drive you to the abominable treason
Of plotting against me, a grisly fate
Awaits you. Feet chained, through the open gate
Of your own flesh you'll suffer, for your sins,
The thrust of radishes and mullets' fins.

Aurelius, father of foodlessness and fast –
And not just this year's hunger, but all past,
Present and future famines – you're mad keen
To have my boy. You make it plain: you're seen
Together, you crack jokes with him, you stick
Close to his side, you're up to every trick.
You'll fail, though: while you're plotting I'll jump in
And dose you with your own foul medicine.
If you had a full belly, I'd keep quiet;
What makes me angry is that from your diet
The wretched boy will get an education
In undernourishment and dehydration.
Hands off, then! Save your honour while you can,
Or you'll end up up-ended, man to man!

24

Juventius, flower of the Juventii,
The sweetest blossom of the family tree –
And I include all present, past and future
Juventii – if you had given that creature
The riches Midas had, I'd feel upset,
But less than I do now watching you let
Yourself be vamped by a fellow who can't claim
A single slave or farthing to his name.

Admirable Veranius and you,
My dear Fabullus, of the retinue
Of the governor Piso – unrewarded rabble
Whose luggage is so empty it's no trouble
To travel with – does it go well or ill
With you these days? Haven't you had your fill
Of shivering and short rations in the train
Of that stale keg? Don't your accounts make plain,
As mine did when a governor was my boss,
That all the gains add up to one big loss?
(O Memmius, you buggered me at your leisure
You raped me to the hilt, you took your pleasure!).
As far as I can see your plight's as bad
As mine was: you've been similarly had
By just as gross a prick. We're both the worse
For chasing high-born 'friends'! May the joint curse
Of all the gods light on them! They disgrace
Romulus, Remus, the whole Roman race.

Dear Ipsitilla, my sweetheart,
My darling, precious, beautiful tart,
Invite me round to be your guest
At noon. Say yes, and I'll request
Another favour: make quite sure
That no one latches the front door,
And don't slip out for a breath of air,
But stay inside, please, and prepare
A love-play with nine long acts in it,
No intervals either! Quick, this minute,
Now, if you're in the giving mood;
For lying here, full of good food,
I feel a second hunger poke
Up through my tunic and my cloak.

We are chaste boys and girls
Devoted to Diana;
Let us now sing our pure
Hymn in Diana's honour.

Latona's child, O great
Daughter of greater Jove,
Whose mother brought you forth
In the Delian olive-grove,

That you should be of all
Hills and loud streams and green
Woods and sequestered glades
The undisputed queen;

Whom women in birth-pangs call
Lucina; also known
As Trivia the witch, or Moon
Whose light is not your own;

Goddess, who month by month
Measures the year's route,

Who crams the farmer's barn
With the earth's good fruit –

Be by what name you please
Invoked, and succour us
As you have ever loved
The race of Romulus.

Paper, please go and ask my chum,
The poet of love Caecilius,
To leave the shore of Larius
And Novum Comum's walls and come
To Verona; for I want to tell
Him several deeply pondered things –
Thoughts of a friend we both know well.
If he's got any sense, he'll eat
The road up, even though that sweet
Girl of his pleads against being parted,
Calls him back countless times and flings
Both arms around his neck. She feels
(If what they tell me is true news)
Desperate with love, head over heels:
For since she's read the poem he's started
On Cybele, fires have been burning,
Gnawing her heart. But I excuse
You, girl, because you're as discerning,
As Sappho as a judge of the Muse.
Yes, the *Great Mother* he's begun
Is so far exquisitely done.

Baboon companions of that nasty inn
Nine posts down from the temple of the twin
Brothers who wear the skull-caps, do you think
That you're the only real men? That we stink,
The rest of us, like goats? That only you
Have the prerogative and the tools to screw
The girls in Rome? Because a hundred strong,
Or two hundred, you sit there in a long
Half-witted row, do you think I wouldn't dare
To bugger the whole lot of you on one chair?
Think what you like; for I intend to scrawl
Obscenities all over your front wall.
For Lesbia, who has broken from my clutch
(And no girl ever will be loved as much
As I loved her), whom I fought other men
Such long, hard battles for, has made your den
Her home. Owners of wealth or a good name,
You're all her lovers now, and, double shame,
So is each half-baked lecher, every randy
Alley cat; at the head of them that dandy,
Egnatius, prince of the long-haired crew,
That son of rabbit-ridden Spain – yes, you
With the two points that make you so alluring:
Thick beard and teeth scrubbed white with Spanish urine.   23

My Cornificius, I'm in distress,
In a bad way, by God my case is grave,
And every hour and day I like it less.
Yet, though you could have with the greatest ease
Offered me comfort, have you done so? Come,
I'm angry now. Is this how friends behave?
Send me a bit of sympathy, any crumb –
Some lines as tender as Simonides'.

Poor Ravidus, is it love-blinded vision
That sends you rushing head-on in collision
With my sharp lines? What god did you invoke
By the wrong words that he should wish to stoke
This red-hot feud of ours? Or can it be
Simply desire for notoriety?
What do you want? A name at any price? Fame?
Then you shall have it, since you've chosen the same
Person to love as I love; for that crime
You'll suffer in this poem for all time.

43

How do you do, girl with the outsize nose,
Colourless eyes, stub fingers, ugly toes,
Coarse conversation and lips none too dry,
Friend of the bankrupt man from Formiae.
Are you the lady whom Cisalpine Gaul
Ranks with my Lesbia and dares to call
Beautiful? O provincial generation –
No taste, no culture, no imagination!

Septimius and Acme were
In love, and he was clasping her.
'Acme, my own,' he said, 'I swear
If I don't love you to despair
And by long years of loving prove
As deep as man can be in love,
Then may I in the desert heat
Of India or Libya meet,
Alone, a green-eyed carnivore!'
At these words Love, who had before
Sneezed on the left-hand side, now sneezed
On the right, to show that he was pleased.

Then Acme gently raised her head
To her sweet boy, and with that red
And rosy mouth of hers she kissed
His eyes swimming with tender mist:
'Darling Septimius, let us serve
This one lord, Love, and never swerve,
Serve him as truly as I claim
That a more passionate, deeper flame
Than yours burns in my heart's soft core!'
At these words Love, who had before

Sneezed on the left-hand side, now sneezed
On the right, to show that he was pleased.

So launched now in auspicious weather,
They sail on, both in love, together,
He, fond fool, happier to hold
His Acme than all Britain's gold
And Syria's perfumes, and she living
Only to please Septimius, giving
Her body's sweets to him alone.
Who in the world has ever known
Such a love-lucky blissful pair
Or Venus' omens set so fair?

48

If someone granted me my fill,
Juventius, of your honey-steeped
Eyes, I should kiss them all day till
I'd reached three hundred thousand and still
Feel hungry to begin again,
Even though the kisses that I reaped
Outnumbered the ripe ears of grain.

To me he seems godlike, in my eyes even
More than divine (if that's not sacrilegious),
The man who sits beside you all day gazing,
    Hearing all day

Your musical laughter. Dazed by love, he loses
The use of all his senses. Oh, the moment
I see you, Lesbia, my voice, throat-strangled,
    Withers away,

My tongue lies paralysed, subtle sensations
Of fire snake through my limbs, my ears are deafened
By their own noise, and, as for eyes, dense darkness
    Blindfolds them both.

Sloth is your enemy, your disease, Catullus;
Your revel in it, crave it, and adore it.
By what else were great kings and flourishing cities
    Ruined but sloth?

52

Why wait, Catullus? Put an end to it,
Die now! To live is to watch Nonius sit
Like a great tumour on the curule chair
And listen to Vatinius forswear
Himself by the consulship he plans to buy.
Why wait, Catullus? Hurry up and die!

Please tell me – that's if you don't mind
me asking – how am I to find
The holes and corners where you hide?
I searched the Lesser Campus, tried
The Circus Maximus and the shrine
Of Jupiter on the Capitoline,
Combed all the bookshops, then waylaid
The girls in Pompey's colonnade,
Begging for you, but met wide-eyed,
Innocent looks on every side.
Desperate, I asked, 'What have you done,
You bad girls, with Camerius?' One,
Teasing me, flaunted a bare breast:
'Here he is, in this rosy nest!'
You keep such a stand-offish distance
That one needs Hercules' persistence
To track you down these days, my friend.
Divulge, disclose where you intend
To be in future; come, commit
Yourself, be reckless, out with it!
Is it that you've spent all day sleeping
Snug in those creamy girls' safe-keeping?
If lips and tongue stay locked and chained,

You waste the whole crop love has gained:
Venus likes speech to be loose-reined.
By all means be discreet – providing
That I'm the one that you confide in.

56

Cato, it's ludicrous, too absurd!
Do listen, it's worth chuckling over.
If you hold Catullus in affection,
Laugh, Cato, for what's just occurred
Is the funniest thing you've ever heard.
I caught a tender little lover,
Bottom up, rogering his bird,
And, brandishing my own erection
(Venus forgive me!), made a third.

57

They make a pretty pair of debauchees,
Sex-sick Mamurra and his bedroom-brother
Caesar. No wonder; they've the same disease
(One caught it in the City and the other
In his own Formiae) and no medicines
Can purge their natures of the ingrown muck.
Pretentious litterateurs, degenerate twins,
Companions of one sofa-bed, they fuck
The girls in friendly rivalry and share
The same unholy itch. A pretty pair!

58

The Lesbia, Caelius, whom in other days
Catullus loved, his great and only love,
My Lesbia, the girl I put above
My own self and my nearest, dearest ones,
Now hangs about crossroads and alleyways
Milking the cocks of mighty Remus' sons.

59

Menenius' wife, Rufa the Bolognese,
Sucks Rufus off. She's the old bag one sees
In cemeteries all the time, beside a grave,
Snatching the food placed on the funeral pyre
And cuffed by the undertaker's half-shaved slave
For chasing loaves that roll out of the fire.

60

Some lioness whelped you on a mountain rock
In Libya, or else you're Scylla's child
Whose womb's all barking dogs; for only a wild
Beast with the nature of a beast could mock
A desperate man making a last appeal
Down on his knees. Bitch heart too hard to feel!

70

She swears she'd rather marry me
Than anyone – even Jupiter,
Supposing he were courting her.
She swears; but what a girl will swear
To the man who loves her ought to be
Scribbled on water, scrawled on air.

I can remember, Lesbia, when you swore
You were mine and mine only, called me more
Desirable than Jove. I loved you then,
And not just in the way that other men
Love mistresses, but as a father cares
For his own sons and daughters, for his heirs.
Now that I know you, you're much cheaper, lighter,
And yet desire in me flares even brighter.
'How can that be?' you say. In love deceit
Freezes affection, though it stokes up heat.

75

Ruined by its own devotion and the great
Wrongs you have done it, Lesbia, to this state
My heart's reduced now: that I'll wish you ill
Though you become a paragon, yet still
Love you, whatever crime you perpetrate.

If there's some pleasure, looking back, in feeling
Conscious of good deeds done to follow men,
Duties performed, promises kept, fair dealing
And no abuse of the name of heaven – why, then,
Catullus, in the life that lies ahead
You have a huge store of enjoyment banked;
For what a friend can say or do you said
And did to help her – and were never thanked;
All the good will you lent was lost on her.
Why let the thought torture you any more?
Toughen your will, be what you once were,
Shrug off the misery that the gods abhor.
It's hard to throw aside love of such long
Standing; it's hard, yet somehow must be done.
There lies your only hope. Whether you're strong
Enough or not, the fight has to be won.
Gods, if you deal in pity, if you lean
Over the dying, easing their last breath,
Look on my trouble and, if mine has been
A pure life, rid me of this plague, this death,
Which creeping through my limbs make me all numb
And drives joy out of me. I've ceased to hope

That she'll return my love, still less become

Faithful, for that's something beyond her scope.
But, Gods, if I have served you, grant my prayer:
Health, and an end to this diseased despair.

Rufus, I thought you were my friend – in vain
And to no end. No end? By God, there was pain
And loss in the end. I felt them when you'd crawled
Into my very guts and, there installed,
Scorched me like arsenic, and like a thief
Snatched away all my happiness. O grief!
O rage! O Rufus, poisonous rust
Of my green life, blight of our friendship's trust!

78

Gallus has brothers; one has a handsome son,
The other a pretty wife. Gallus is clever
And *so* sophisticated. Just for fun
He tucks the lovely pair in bed together.
Gallus is stupid. No wise husband teaches
A nephew how to fill his uncle's breeches.

78b

. . . What pains me most is that your spittle-slime
Has fouled my sweet girl's sweet lips. But the crime
Is one you'll have to pay for, for your shame
Shall echo down the centuries, and Fame
Grow old and ugly muttering your name.

79

Pulcer means 'handsome', and why not? He's well
Named, for his sister Lesbia loves his face
Far more than me and all my kin. And yet
I give good-looking Pulcer leave to sell
Me and all mine as slaves if he can get
Three decent friends to suffer his embrace.

81

Is there no nice young fellow in the whole
City to fall in love with that you pick
This stranger with a face as pale and sick
As a gilded statue, bred in that plague-hole
Pisaurum – whom you've made your favourite
And had the insolence to place above
Me? Oh, Juventius, are you blind, through love,
To the crime against good taste that you commit?

82

If you'd have Catullus owe his eyes to you,
Or something dearer than his eyes, then do
Him a favour, Quintius. Hands off what's to him
Dearer than eyes, dearer than life or limb.

83

When Lesbia's husband's there, she never fails
To say hard things about me, and they please
The silly man. Mule, are you deaf and blind?
If she kept quiet, having put me from her mind,
She would be properly cured of her disease.
But, as it is, the way she snarls and rails
Proves she remembers, and, what's worse, the pique
Infuriates her. She burns, so she *must* speak.

85

I hate and love. If you aske me to explain
    The contradiction,
I can't, but I can feel it, and the pain
    Is crucifixion.

Many think Quintia's beautiful. She's tall
And well-proportioned and her skin is white.
I grant her these good points, but I won't call
Her 'beautiful'. She has one fatal fault –
No sex-appeal: there's not a grain of salt
In that big dish to stir the appetite.
Lesbia *is* beautiful – not only blessed
With better looks than other girls, but dressed
In the mystery she's stolen from the rest.

87

No woman can
Truthfully aver
That any man
Ever loved her
As I loved you.

No lover bound
By pledge of heart
Was ever found
True on his part
As I was true.

88

Gellius, would you say it was right
For a man to monkey around all night
With his mother and sister, half undressed?
Or to cuckoo his uncle's marital nest?
How much guilt does he bear? Far more
Than Tethys washing her farthest shore
Or Ocean, daddy of nymphs, can clean.
He couldn't do anything more obscene,
Not even if, head between his legs,
He took a swig of his own foul dregs.

From Gellius' and his mother's vile
Incestuous union let there spring
A Magus who in Persian style
Will learn the art of soothsaying;
For son and mother must conceive
A Magus out of their perversion
(At least if one is to believe
The blasphemous doctrine of the Persian),
And then their misbegotten brat
Can please his gods with songs of praise,
Watching the greasy entrail-fat
Melt in the sacrificial blaze.

The reason, Gellius, why I picked on you
In those heart-breaking, aching days to trust
Was not because I'd tried and proved you true
Or thought you capable of restraining lust,
But that the girl I loved was neither sister
Nor mother of yours; and, though I'd known you long,
I hoped that you'd find cause there to resist a
Temptation to do mischief. I was wrong:
You found no cause at all, so much you revel
In anything that smacks of filth and evil.

92

Lesbia spits all day against my name,
And yet I'll stake my life she loves me. Why?
I curse her all the time – I've just the same
Symptoms. If I don't love her, let me die.

So help me God, I couldn't choose between
Smelling Aemilius head-on or behind:
His mouth and arse are equally unclean.
Well, no, perhaps the latter's more refined,
Being toothless; for the mouth shows yard-long teeth,
Gums like a worn-out cart-frame with parts missing,
And a grin that stretches like the cunt beneath
An old mule on a hot day when she's pissing.
He fucks the girls and fancies he's got charm.
Why don't we post him to the grinding-wheel
To drive the donkeys on a penal farm?
As for a woman who's prepared to feel
Aemilius, she'd fondle a diseased
Hangman and lick him anywhere he pleased.

Juventius, my honey, while you played
I stole a little kiss from you. It was
Sweeter than sweet ambrosia. I paid
The penalty, though; for, nailed to the high cross
Of your displeasure, I remember spending
More than an hour feebly excusing it,
While all the tears I shed for the offending
Act didn't soften your fierce mood one bit.
As soon as it was done you washed the place
With water, then you wiped it with each finger
In turn, meticulously, just in case
Any contagion from my mouth might linger –
As though you'd been infected on the lips
By some foul whore's saliva! Now, moreover,
You've sentenced me to the racks, the screws, the whips
Reserved by Love for the tormented lover;
So that, ambrosial once, that kiss became
Bitterer than the bitterest hellebore.
If that's the sort of punishment you claim,
I shan't steal kisses from you any more.

100

Two fine young men, the flower of all Verona,
Are sick with love, one for a girl, the other
Mad for a boy – Quintius for Aufillena,
Caelius for Aufillenus, who's her brother.
Well, here's a loving partnership that lends
A new twist to 'the brotherhood of friends'!
Who gets my vote? You, Caelius, who've shown
True friendship, tried and tested in the fire
When my wild passion burnt me to the bone.
Caelius, good luck! All power to your desire!

Do you think I could have ever cast a slur
On the girl who's dearer to me than both eyes?
Not possible. Nor would I, if it were,
Be, as I am, half-mad with love for her.
Oh, you and Tappo dream up monstrous lies!

106

Seeing a pretty boy with an auctioneer,
What does one think? 'He's up for sale – and dear'.

To long and long, then unexpectedly
To have one's wish is the true crown of pleasure;
And so I find, now you've returned to me,
My Lesbia, my more than golden treasure –
Brought yourself back of your own sweet accord,
Hopelessly longed for, beyond hope restored.
Chalk up a white mark for this lucky day!
Does any man alive enjoy such bliss
As I have? Is it possible to say
There's anything in life better than this?

109

My dear, you promise that this love we both
Feel will be everlastingly contented.
Great gods, make sure that she can prove her oath
And that she spoke the truth and truly meant it,
That we may keep in our time, and beyond
All time, this love's inviolable bond.

Good mistresses are praised: they take their hire
And honour their side of the bargain later.
You, Aufillena, cheat me, you're a liar,
Not half as much a lover as a hater;
    You like to take and never give –
    And that's a vicious way to live.

An honest woman would by now have kept
Her promise (a nice girl would never make it);
But, Aufillena, greedily to accept
Presents to seal a contract and then break it
    Puts you below the grasping whore;
    She pays the flesh that's haggled for.